Thank Heaven for Little Girls

A Celebration in Words and Pictures

Text by Sister Carol Ann Nawracaj
Photographs by Monica Rich Kosann

Published by
Adams Media Corporation
260 Center Street, Holbrook, MA 02343, U.S.A.
www.adamsmedia.com

ISBN: 1-58062-281-X

Printed in Canada

J I H G F E D C B A

Library of Congress Cataloging-in-Publication Data
Nawracaj, Carol Ann.
Thank heaven for little girls : a celebration in words and pictures / text by
Sister Carol Ann Nawracaj ; photographs by Monica Rich Kosann.
    p.   cm.
ISBN 1-58062-281-X
1. Girls. 2. Girls--Pictorial works. I. Title.
HQ777 .N38   2001
305.23--dc21   00-049609

This publication is designed to provide accurate and authoritative information with regard to the subject matter covered. It is sold with the understanding that the publisher is not engaged in rendering legal, accounting, or other professional advice. If legal advice or other expert assistance is required, the services of a competent professional person should be sought.

— From a *Declaration of Principles* jointly adopted by a Committee of the
American Bar Association and a Committee of Publishers and Associations

This book is available at quantity discounts for bulk purchases.
For information, call 1-800-872-5627.

Cover and interior photographs by Monica Rich Kosann.
Copyright continues with permissions on page 90.

DEDICATIONS

This book is affectionately dedicated to my mother, with gratitude and love for being the most influential woman in my life and to my sister, Terri, with enduring love and admiration for being my best friend.

—Sister Carol Ann Nawracaj

*   *   *

This book is for my girls.

—Monica Rich Kosann

TABLE OF CONTENTS

Introduction 1

A Time for Being 13

A Time for Loving 29

A Time for Growing 41

A Time for Becoming 53

A Time for Blossoming 81

INTRODUCTION

On a recent Sunday afternoon, Monica Rich Kosann, my partner in the development of this book, visited a local bookstore with her daughters. As they had done on so many prior occasions, the children went off to explore their own areas of interest, individually

> *One can never consent to creep when one feels an impulse to soar.*
> HELEN KELLER, *THE STORY OF MY LIFE*

browsing shelves or sitting quietly with a book of their choice. Close to an hour later, as Monica attempted to gather her two daughters for a soccer game, she found one of them seated on the floor in an aisle of books, engrossed in her selection and oblivious to the demands of the clock. Wondering what subject had captured her imagination, Monica stooped beside her and asked what she was reading.

"It's a book of inventions," said her daughter, thumbing through the pages of a large book describing inventions through the ages. She told Monica about the wheel, Gutenberg's printing press, Galileo's telescope, Alexander Graham Bell's telephone, Edison's light bulb, and kept right

You may give [children] your love but not your thoughts,
For they have their own thoughts.
You may house their bodies but not their souls,
For their souls dwell in the house of tomorrow.
KAHLIL GIBRAN, *THE PROPHET*

3

on going through the silicon chip and the personal computer.

"The only problem," she added, "is that I want to be an inventor and scientist, but it seems all the people in this book are men." She paused. "Is that a problem?"

Monica marveled at her daughter's question and the pure inquisitiveness so often found in many children. Sometimes it takes the keen insight of a child to articulate something as complex as the changing role of women as simply as, "Is that a problem?"

Mama exhorted her children at every opportunity to "jump at de sun." We might not land on the sun, but at least we would get off the ground.
ZORA NEALE HURSTON, *DUST TRACKS ON A ROAD*

Monica explained
that it most definitely was
not a problem. She told her
daughter that Madame Curie
was also one of the pioneers
of modern science, and
that countless women had
changed the face of science,
technology, and engineering,
often going on to start
computer software businesses
and the like. Her daughter

She is more precious than rubies,
and all the things that you may
desire cannot compare with her.
PROVERBS 3:15

5

smiled broadly. "I will be like Madame Curie," she declared. Then she folded the book under her arm and walked off to the cashier.

How different are this young Madame Curie's dreams from those of young girls of previous generations—when the limits to a young girl's future were set not by her imagination but by the world around her? In the past, how many young girls were challenged to *go beyond* our expectations? How often were they given the opportunity to step into new roles—in education, business, the arts, politics—even as Supreme Court justices or secretaries of state?

You may have similar hopes and dreams of an unlimited future for the little girls in your life—a vision of a world where the only limit to their accomplishments would be the boundaries of their own imaginations.

> *If we build on a sure foundation in friendship, we must love our friends for their own sakes rather than our own.*
> CHARLOTTE BRONTË

Each day provides its own gifts.
MARTIAL, EPIGRAMS

By challenging our young girls to pursue their dreams, to enter uncharted waters, we can help them build their self-confidence and their futures.

When Monica and I developed our first book, *Treasures from Heaven*, we celebrated what we called the "Gift of Children"—gifts of life, trust, wonder, discovery, happiness, love, and friendship. Among these gifts, we identified the unbridled optimism of children and their ability to continually remind us of what is truly important in our daily lives. It was this very optimism that Monica saw in the face of her daughter at that bookstore—optimism about the future, which for her would now represent a time of unlimited potential.

*Keep your face to the sunshine
and you cannot see the shadows.*
HELEN KELLER

It was not long after that afternoon when Monica and I decided to work together on this book, to continue our celebration of children. This time we chose to focus on girls and girlhood. We wanted to celebrate the challenges, developments, and life experiences that define young girls on their path to becoming women.

As the popular verse from Ecclesiastes reminds us:

There is a time for everything: a time to be born . . . a time to plant; a time to harvest; . . . a time to heal; . . . a time to cry; a time to laugh; . . . a time to be quiet; a time to speak; a time for loving; . . . a time for peace.

As little girls make their wondrous journeys to womanhood, they truly need time for being, for loving, for growing, for becoming, and for blossoming—time to continue the journey of boundless optimism that they have already begun.

Who would ever think that so much can go on in the soul of a young girl.
ANNE FRANK

The essence of this book is our celebration of their journeys. As we look upon the beautiful girls in the pages ahead, we must remember our responsibility to nourish the uninhibited hope and curiosity that turn the innocent ambitions of girlhood into the accomplishments of womanhood. ✳

Some minds seem almost to create themselves, springing up under every disadvantage and working their solitary but irresistible way through a thousand obstacles.
WASHINGTON IRVING, *THE SKETCH BOOK*

A TIME FOR BEING

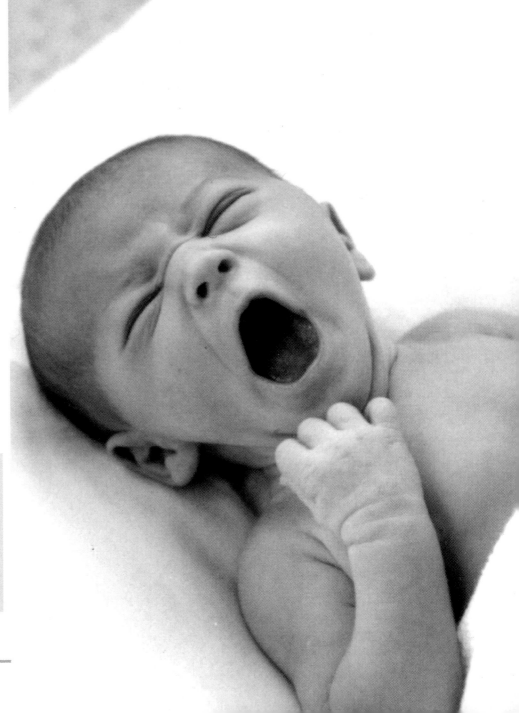

W hat is a little girl? Some picture a delightful, ethereal infant clothed in pink lace and frills, her head nestled comfortably on her mother's shoulder, her tiny hands

Dear, dear! How queer everything is today!
And yesterday things went on just as usual.
I wonder if I've changed in the night? Let me
think: was I the same when I got up this morning?
I almost think I can remember feeling a little different.
But if I'm not the same, the next question is,
"Who in the world am I?" Ah, that's the great puzzle.
LEWIS CARROLL, *ALICE'S ADVENTURES IN WONDERLAND*

exploring her face and spontaneously reaching for those shiny glasses that promise an adventure. Just by lying in her crib, gurgling with joy or fretting for a change, she evokes our tenderness and care.

At any age, the aura that surrounds a little girl is a beacon of light. Her pixie-like activity elicits cheery smiles, touches weary hearts, and lifts heavy spirits. Her very presence, inviting all to join in her song and dance, evokes joy. Scampering down the grocery aisle, playing hopscotch on the pavement, dressing up for make-believe, running through the city park, bicycling with Mom and Dad—no matter where she is or what she does, a girl's very being invites attention.

One cannot help but love the little girls that cross our paths. They can be a source of wonder and of immense delight, if only we can learn to see and appreciate the magic of their innocence.

He nurtured and taught her; he guarded her as the apple of his eye.
DEUTERONOMY 32:10

Sometimes little girls are at their most beautiful when they just act naturally. A friend of mine was on vacation with her relatives, and the adults had gathered in the living room, engaged in small talk. Their discussion was interrupted when the hosts' two-year-old daughter, who had just awakened from her nap, entered down the stairway. Everyone gazed with awe and delight as this little cherub descended the steps with unstudied ease—no Miss

You are the fairest of all.
PSALM 45:2

She walks in beauty, like the night
Of cloudless climes and starry skies;
And all that's best of dark and bright
Meet in her aspect and her eyes.
LORD BYRON, *SHE WALKS IN BEAUTY*

17

America ever walked on stage with so much grace and poise, or with such a pleasant natural smile.

What makes a little girl so lovable? Her very existence invites a love that is hard to resist! Love is an inseparable part of who she is! She presents a picture of beauty and grace, sweetness and playfulness, as her laughter giggles its way into our unsuspecting hearts. A charmer by nature, she delights all with whom she

A rosy, chubby, sunshiny little soul was Daisy, who found her way to everybody's heart, and nestled there, one of the captivating children, who seem made to be kissed and cuddled, adorned and adored like little goddesses, and produced for general approval on all festive occasions. Her small virtues were so sweet that she would have been quite angelic if a few small naughtinesses had not kept her delightfully human.
LOUISA MAY ALCOTT, *LITTLE WOMEN*

comes into contact. Her very being shouts "LOVE" out loud!

And who can be as creative as a little girl? When you were growing up, you may have entertained yourself with hopscotch, jumping rope, and playing board games the way today's girls play with Barbies® and computer games. But it doesn't take expensive toys to

Her father called her "Little Tranquility," and the name suited her excellently; for she seemed to live in a happy world of her own, only venturing out to meet the few whom she trusted and loved.
LOUISA MAY ALCOTT, LITTLE WOMEN

19

delight and spark a little girl's imagination. I've always been fascinated by how much she can do with very little. She can weave magic from ordinary things—conjuring up her own world of characters from spoons and forks, stones and branches, bottle tops and rubber bands—whatever is at hand.

She can make a palace out of a backyard, a royal family of her dolls, and can create a hundred different ways to play the same game. Her playmates are toys and flowers and butterflies, and if one is lucky enough to pass by, then one is joyfully welcomed into her world. As much as she delights others, she also takes delight in all that surrounds her. She makes life come alive when she's around. The sun is brighter; colors are more vivid; life is just grand!

Little girls can work miracles in our lives. A neighbor who had recently become a father remarked, "No person, no event could ever

The girl was lovely to behold.
ESTHER 2:7

21

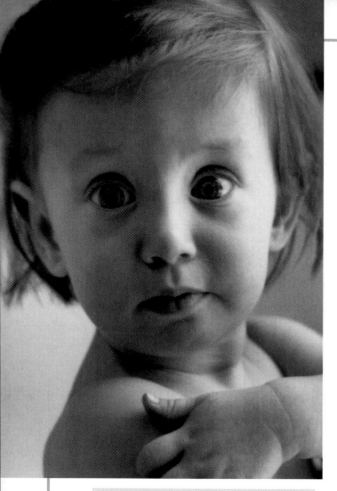

get me up at three in the morning. But now, for my baby daughter, I'd do anything!"

How many times have you said—or heard others say—the same thing? "My precious little girl is the best part of my life." "She has given my life meaning." "My daughter is going to the best schools even if I have to mortgage our house." Comments like these are too numerous to count, for sure!

One man said this about his own radical conversion: "When our little girl was born, like

any proud father, I believed that our baby was the loveliest girl in the world. I wanted her to be a good girl. Then it dawned on me that I could not just *wish* her to be good, but that I had to set a positive example. Whatever I did, or did not do, would affect her. I suddenly realized that I wasn't pleased with my own lifestyle. I turned my life around 180 degrees for my little girl's sake. Her arrival on this earth made a good father, a good person, out of me."

With the introduction of a little girl's feminine innocence, most parents experience a greater motivation to be more patient, more gentle, more trustworthy, more responsible—more of everything that turns good parents into better people. Truly, a little girl performs miracles.

Every little girl is as unique as each star in the galaxy, each grain of sand, each twinkle in a parent's eye. It is this very uniqueness that makes her who she is, and it must be cultured, treasured, and reverenced.

A friend is a person with whom I may be sincere.
Before [her] I may think aloud.
RALPH WALDO EMERSON

25

Like so many girls today, the girls or daughters in your life may be active in sports, and the clothing they wear—hockey jerseys, football jerseys, and basketball tank tops—may reflect their interest. To some, these clothes may seem like a radical departure from the pink lace and frills worn by many young girls. Friends and grownups might even suggest

How do I love thee? Let me count the ways.
I love thee to the death and breadth and height
My soul can reach . . .
ELIZABETH BARRETT BROWNING, *SONNETS FROM THE PORTUGUESE*

Life is mostly froth and bubble,
Two things stand like stone,
Kindness in another's trouble,
Courage in your own.
ADAM LINDSAY GORDON, *Ye Wearie Wayfarer*

that these "boy" clothes are inappropriate! You can remind the girls in your life that their choice of clothing is simply one more way they can express themselves, and that it's such choices that make each of us special and unique.

I remember how touched I was when I heard a little girl consoling her sister on the playground. The boys were playing ball and the little girl was eager to join in the game. The boys did not share her enthusiasm and refused to

27

We can do no great things—
only small things with great love.
MOTHER TERESA

allow her to play with them. She cried and, seeking comfort, told her story to her sister. Her sister's reply helped ease her disappointment: "That's okay, Susie. They won't let you play because they know you are better than they are, and that you'll beat them at their own game!" The little girl smiled, dried her eyes, and ran to another group of children to play.

A little girl is a wonderfully rare gift to all. It is not the color of her hair or eyes or the shape of her face or nose that makes her so special. It is the twinkle in her eyes, the lovely little gestures she makes, the special laughter that erupts at unpredictable times—all the things that make *her* who *she* is that captures our attention and captivates our hearts. ✳

A TIME FOR LOVING

I was on the playground at my school, enjoying my conversation with a few of the children. As we spoke, two usually polite little girls kept bumping into me. After a few collisions, it became clear that they weren't going to apologize, either! Feeling a

> *A friend may well be reckoned the masterpiece of nature.*
> RALPH WALDO EMERSON, "FRIENDSHIP,"
> *ESSAYS: FIRST SERIES*

little annoyed by their behavior, I decided to remind them of their manners. The two little girls stared at me in surprise and explained, "But, Sister, we're playing tag—and you're the base!"

Chuckling to myself, I realized that I should have been honored by their comfort with me.

Loving relationships are built on a foundation of this kind of security and trust. When an infant grasps this, she leans naturally towards others and offers herself in a tender embrace. Her delight in discovering new things and new people emanates from a place deep within. She cannot help but love!

With one hand holding onto her family, she reaches with her other hand toward those who enter her circle. Thus it is then, early in life, when young girls start to treasure the "other." The

> *Friends are born, not made.*
> HENRY BROOK ADAMS,
> *THE EDUCATION OF HENRY ADAMS*

very games they learn and create are relationship oriented. "You be the daddy. I'll be the mommy."

This need for sharing, for loving and being loved by another, is evident in a story told about my niece. Outspoken even at the age of five, she announced that she was lonely as an only child—and wanted a sister! She listed all the fun they would do together: play games and dress up, make crafts, share secrets, etc. In conclusion, she added, "Oh, yes, and she must be five years old."

Those friends thou hast, their adoption tried,
Grapple them to thy soul with hoops of steel.
WILLIAM SHAKESPEARE, *HAMLET*

Forsake not an old friend; for the
new is not comparable to [her].
ECCLESIASTES 9:10

Your loving influence—your willingness to give, share, and demonstrate your love—contributes to the ease and comfort with which a girl makes her journey to womanhood. Whether it's participating in a silly game or just listening to their problems, little girls need a loving "base" they can rely on.

Demonstrating love does not require dramatic action. A young girl learns how to love others by observing you holding a door for the person

Be a friend to thyself, and others will be so too.
THOMAS FULLER, GNOMOLOGIA

behind you, being polite in word and manner, picking up an object that someone has dropped. What is important is that she is eager to learn from your example, and enjoys the experience of giving of herself.

Being loved freely and spontaneously makes it possible for a young girl to

There is no friend like a sister
In calm or stormy weather:
To cheer one on the tedious way,
To fetch one if one goes astray,
To strengthen whilst one stands.
CHRISTINA ROSSETTI

reciprocate with her personal kind of love. With her parents' example as her base, a young girl can create special relationships with her peers and siblings, bonding heart-to-heart in unspoken commitment to another.

Many of our most lasting friendships develop early in life. Passing a playground full of happy and excited children, one can easily see relationships forming. Sitting on a bench with heads bowed close to each other, playing skip rope, jacks, or hopscotch, walking hand in hand around the yard, giggling in a corner or under a tree—little girls bond with each other so quickly. And one can't even begin to imagine what they share!

The loving base my parents provided manifests itself in my relationship with my sister, Terri. Since there is a seven-year difference in our ages, and I entered the convent when she entered the second grade, you might predict that we wouldn't have much in common. On the contrary—we are so alike,

Is solace anywhere more comforting than in the arms of a sister?
ALICE WALKER

it is incredible. It is common for me to purchase a birthday card for someone in our family and learn that Terri has purchased the exact same card—even though we are miles apart. One Mother's Day, we purchased the same card *and* the same gift.

The invisible bond I share with my sister certainly runs

I shall pass through this world but once.
If therefore there is any kindness I can show,
or any good thing I can do, let me do it now;
let me not defer or neglect it.
ATTRIBUTED TO ETIENNE DE GRELLETT

deep within us. When encouraged and nurtured, the love between family members provides an irreplaceable and essential support network that helps transform little girls into responsible, loving women.

The greatest gift a child can receive is unconditional love. It is the basis upon which one's concept of self is built and one's self-esteem is nurtured. It is this love that generates love in return. When nurtured with such love,

Expressed affection is the best of all methods to use when you want to light a glow in someone's heart and to feel it in your own.
RUTH STAFFORD PEALE

a young girl views life as exciting and challenging. She dares to dream and enjoys the experience of who she is and of who she would like to be.

Love, indeed, is the base from which all flows and to which all returns. Teach a little girl to love and she will return it beyond measure!✳

No act of kindness, no matter how small, is ever wasted.
AESOP, *THE LION AND THE MOUSE*

A TIME FOR GROWING

When I was about five years old, I remember emptying the pots and pans from my mom's cupboard to create a neat place to play. I also enjoyed playing supermarket in her kitchen. I'd line up all the chairs and fill them with canned goods and other items from her cupboards. With a large crayon, I'd scribble the prices

How to eat spinach like a child. Divide into piles. Rearrange again into piles. After five or six maneuvers, sit back and say you are full.
DELIA EPHRON, *NEW YORK TIMES*

on pieces of brown bags. A friend and I would take turns being the grocer, and we'd use play money from other games to pay for our purchases. What I remember most, though, is not how much fun we had playing that game, but that my mom never scolded us for messing up her kitchen—she was happy to see us enjoy ourselves so much!

On a given day, a girl's daydreams can lead her onstage thrilling her many admirers or behind the scenes making things happen. She may see herself as a ballerina and popular singer, a figure skater or an Olympic hopeful, a loving mother and business executive, an artist or a composer. Infinite possibilities beckon her—and she delights in discovering that so many avenues are open to her.

Her world offers an open invitation to be whatever or whomever she chooses, because of the love and support she's received from her parents and others. She has learned that she is special, and this knowledge gives her identity that grows into self-awareness and self-acceptance.

> "Th' more they laugh th' better for 'em!" said Mrs. Sowerby, still laughing herself. "Good, healthy child laughin's better than pills any day o' th' year..."
> FRANCES HODGSON BURNETT, THE SECRET GARDEN

My students once visited the mayor's office on a field trip. The students were very attentive as the mayor explained the symbolism of the city's flag, took them on a tour of the offices, and led them through a simulation of an emergency situation. Finally, we arrived at his office where we viewed his many awards, photographs with the president and other government officials, and other memorabilia. Prominently displayed was a photograph of our students taken with the mayor when he had visited the school a few months earlier.

Children's games are hardly games. Children are never more serious than when they play.
MONTAIGNE, *ESSAYS*

I care not so much what I am in the opinion of others, as what I am in my own; I would be rich of myself, and not by borrowing.
MONTAIGNE, *ESSAYS*

When I pointed the photo out to the girls, I was surprised at how they seemed to take it for granted.

Upon returning to the school, I voiced my disappointment to the other teachers. One remarked, "I don't see why you're surprised. After all, it's your own fault!" Dumbfounded, I asked her why. "Well," she explained, "you tell the students they're 'special' so often that they probably *expected* to see their photograph in the mayor's office."

A little girl's image of herself is the result of our continual positive reinforcement. She grows into self-awareness and self-esteem

Curiosity is one of the permanent and certain characteristics of a vigorous mind.
SAMUEL JOHNSON, *THE RAMBLER*

through the approval and support we provide. More importantly, our affirmations take root deep inside—and finally become an integral part of her life.

Throughout her infancy and early childhood, a little girl is often affirmed merely for who she is as a person. As a passage from the Book of Ruth states, "Thank God for a girl like you." That is how my parents made me feel every day!

"Curiouser and curiouser!" cried Alice.
LEWIS CARROLL, *ALICE'S ADVENTURES IN WONDERLAND*

47

I remember my mom telling me about the day of my birth. Dad came home from work that day with a beautiful heart-shaped box full of dark chocolates. "Happy Valentine's Day, Hon," he said as he handed it to her. "Take me to the hospital," she replied. I entered the world at three o'clock the next morning!

Ever since then, Dad always brought Mom a large heart-shaped box of chocolates on Valentine's Day—and then presented me with a smaller one. Once he included a card that read: "To the most wonderful woman in my life . . . next to Mommy."

As a girl grows older, she'll get approval from her peers—and from teachers, relatives, and other adults—on many different levels. "Wow! What a great pitch!" "I love your new shoes." "Where'd you get that neat game?" "That's awesome!" "I didn't know you could do that!" "Your report was really good!"

Never be afraid to sit awhile and think.
LORRAINE HANSBERRY, *A RAISIN IN THE SUN*

When you make little girls feel special, they respond by *becoming* special. Girls will see themselves as competent and worthy if they're treated that way. They'll begin to believe in themselves and in their capacity to grow through learning and loving.

Our image of just what a little girl can do is constantly changing—and growing—as they expand their world, their interests, and their possibilities. Twenty years ago, who could have predicted that millions of young girls would identify with the dynamic women on the United States soccer team that won the World Cup? As

Who has self-confidence will lead the rest.
HORACE, *EPISTLES*

those women led their team to victory, they helped a generation of girls redefine their hopes, aspirations, beauty, and grace in exciting new directions.

Expect great things of girls and they will often deliver great things. We need to remind them that, someday, *their* pictures could be on television or in a magazine describing their latest triumph or discovery. As Eleanor Roosevelt once remarked, "The future belongs to those who believe in the beauty of their dreams." If we believe in the dreams of the young girls in our lives, they will share the same conviction. If we raise girls to be self-assured and happy with themselves, we will be rewarded by their magnificent accomplishments as they grow and develop into confident young women. ✳

A TIME FOR BECOMING

How charming to see a four-year-old girl covered up to her elbows with flour because she wants to make Daddy his very own cookies. Or running for her toy sweeper so that she can help Mommy clean the house. She learns about fashion

We do not need, and indeed never will have, all the answers before we act.... It is often only through taking action that we can discover some of them.

CHARLOTTE BUNCH, "NOT BY DEGREE," *PASSIONATE POLITICS*

from dressing her dolls and playing with cutouts, and soon she is creating her own fashions with brilliant colors and styles.

A girl's first teacher is often her mother. She teaches not only the basics of reading, writing, and arithmetic; but the common courtesies of letting elders have a seat, holding the door open for someone, saying the magic words "please" and "thank you," along with the skills of balancing work and family, and playing an active role in community life. Whether in dreaming up adventures or reading from a book, a mother hands down the important values of life—honesty, integrity, kindness, caring, responsibility, and a work ethic— and is always inspiring and motivating.

As I look back on my childhood years, I appreciated the sacrifices my mother made for the benefit of my family and how she always put the family's needs, wants, and dreams ahead of her own. My mother demonstrated unconditional love,

How far that little candle throws its beams!
WILLIAM SHAKESPEARE, *THE MERCHANT OF VENICE*

We were a club, a society, a civilization all our own.
Annette Funicello, Original Mouseketeer

patience, and understanding in everything she did, from baking special birthday cakes to sewing doll clothes to driving me to school.

Women, especially mothers, play an invaluable role in the development of young girls. Mothers teach their daughters a wealth of knowledge and skills, as well as a way of being—one that is productive, compassionate, and supportive—that they can pass along to their own daughters.

As adults, we bring our young girls to the edge of so many new experiences, try to put them on the right path, watch them test boundaries, experiment, and move forward.

To be simple is the best thing in the world; to be modest is the next best thing. I am not sure about being quiet.
G.K. Chesterton, All Things Considered

How many times do girls approach the edge of a new learning experience, back away for a moment, sure that they can't succeed, then forge ahead to emerge victorious?

For little girls, everyday life offers a host of new ideas, experiences, and behaviors from which they can learn. It acts as a solid beginning for their process of becoming—opening new vistas for them every day. New experiences provide an invaluable starting point for developing character in young children. From their experiences, they learn to experiment, to think about the consequences of

Grown-ups never understand anything for themselves, and it is tiresome for children to be always and forever explaining things to them.
SAINT-EXUPÉRY, THE LITTLE PRINCE

their actions, to realize that there are alternatives and choices, to develop individual styles and opinions, and to risk a friendship for the truth. If we demonstrate our values in a loving manner, young girls will learn to incorporate them into their own lives.

Integrity, honesty, and strength of character are values built on trust and love. How many of us can share a personal story of not being

Nothing happens unless first you dream.
CARL SANDBURG

59

punished by our parents for having made a mistake? And what did we learn from those experiences—and how our parents responded?

Whether it's torn clothing, misplaced toys, or misused articles of Mommy's clothing, every little girl will make mistakes. While these setbacks may seem life threatening to her at the time, a little girl discovers how to learn from her experiences through her parent's forgiveness and support.

I remember a young girl telling me that she felt good about herself because her parents loved and trusted her to do the right thing. She had discovered that life is full of challenges—but also that she could make a mistake and learn from it. Most important, she learned that her parents would be there to listen to her, guide her, and enable her to be who she is.

Vision is the art of seeing things invisible.
Jonathan Swift

She recalled that when she was a little girl, she took lipstick from her mother's bureau, smeared it on her lips and cheeks, and went to the telephone to have an engaging conversation with an operator. Her mother must have chuckled at the sight, and without reprimanding her, spoke to the operator, replaced the phone on its cradle, and took her to wash off the telltale stains. The next day her mom gave her a tube of little girls' lipstick. She was so proud!

When I was a young girl I loved to draw. Once, my mom bought a pair of blue shoes and a bottle of blue shoe polish to keep them looking

new. I soon discovered that the blue polish was better than any blue paint I had, and the applicator could cover a wider area in a lot quicker time than my small paintbrush.

Without asking permission, I "borrowed" my mom's blue shoe polish and began working on a picture in our basement. Unfortunately, I accidentally spilled some of the blue shoe polish. My efforts to clean up the mess resulted in the spot getting larger and larger. Since I couldn't remove it, I decided to cover my crime with a large metal tub.

A few days passed before I finally had the courage to tell my mom about my accident—only to learn that she had been aware of it all the time. After all, that large tub in the middle of the floor must have been obvious. I appreciated that she didn't scold me for my actions—or try to stifle my creative energies.

One cannot have too large a party.
JANE AUSTEN, *EMMA*

Every young girl encounters her own problems. How she tackles the obstacles that life presents defines who she is, and who she will be. We need to help her understand and rejoice in the unique solutions she offers.

One little girl shared with me her solution to a problem she encountered with her siblings and a puzzle. Her brothers and sisters loved putting jigsaw puzzles together, but each wanted to be the

You are the bows from which your children are as living arrows sent forth.
KAHLIL GIBRAN, *THE PROPHET*

If it is to be, it is up to me.
SHIRLEY HUTTON

one to put the last piece in place. Her brilliant idea? "Why don't we all take one piece from the puzzle before we start and put it in a safe place. Then when we come to the end we can all have a last piece to put in together!" Quite ingenious of her! She had learned that the best solutions are often those that encompass everyone's needs.

A friend of mine shared the story of how his younger daughter learned to deal with her frustrations with her older sister. One day, as can so often happen with siblings,

his daughter was upset over her sister's unwillingness to let her borrow something. Following her father's advice, she approached her sister quietly, calmly, and gently, explaining why she should lend her the object in question. Minutes later she returned with the item in hand, her strategy a success. Her frustration was replaced by happiness, and they were best of friends again. The quiet calm of her approach had dissolved their confrontation.

Listening and learning to see a situation through someone else's perspective, especially a close friend's, will help a girl through the myriad problems she is bound to face along the path to becoming a confident, self-assured person.

One day, close to dismissal time, a young girl approached me to discuss a problem. I would have preferred to wait until the following morning but, after listening to her, I realized it could not wait! I keep a

My sister taught me everything I really need to know, and she was only in the sixth grade at the time.
LINDA SUNSHINE

Parents can only give advice or put them on the right paths, but the final forming of a person's character lies in their own hands.

ANNE FRANK, *THE DIARY OF A YOUNG GIRL*

small smooth stone in my office desk to remind me to see things through the eyes of a child. We discussed that her problem was like that small stone: it may look big if you put it right next to your eye, but just as she could place that small stone on the floor and step over it, so, too, would she be able to "step over" her problem.

A social worker once brought two girls, normally good friends, into my office after an altercation. It was obvious that the girls were reluctant to discuss the matter.

To give them some time to simmer down, I reached for a glass with a sport logo stenciled on it. A crumpled piece of tissue paper had been placed inside to block the view through the glass.

I asked one girl whose logo she saw on the glass. "The Giants," came her quick reply. I asked the other girl the same question. She shot back, "The 49ers."

I removed the crumpled paper and slowly turned the glass 180 degrees. Then I asked them both, "Which one of you is correct?" The design on the glass contained *both* logos. Which you saw depended on which side you were looking at.

Experience is the best teacher.
WILL ROGERS, ILLITERATE DIGEST

As both girls sat in silence, I asked them to ponder what had happened and left the room. When I returned one of the girls remarked, "You know, Sister, we really are good friends and we want to thank you for giving us an opportunity to talk this out."

Learning how to see a situation from someone else's perspective can be an invaluable learning experience for a little girl!

Overcoming barriers, though often painful to endure, is another key part of a young girl's growing process.

I am the master of my fate
I am the captain of my soul.
W.E. HENLEY, *INVITUS*

One holiday season a recent newcomer to our school, a bright young girl, was cast in the lead role of "Marie" in our production of *The Nutcracker*. At first she reluctantly accepted the part, but happily gained confidence with each rehearsal. When opening night arrived, she was a smashing success,

She stared out of the window at the passing people with a queer old-fashioned thoughtfulness in her big eyes.... She was always dreaming and thinking odd things and could not herself remember any time when she had not been thinking things about grown-up people and the world they belong to.
FRANCES HODGSON BURNETT, *A LITTLE PRINCESS*

73

and of course she was euphoric when she heard loud applause from everyone—her parents, peers, teachers, and the entire audience!

Later, backstage, she recalled the reason for her original reluctance to be the leading lady. She said, "In my old school I was never given a part like this. All I ever was—was a brick." That evening was clearly her time not to be a brick, but to be the self-confident lead in a beautiful performance. Sometimes all it takes is the opportunity!

Sometimes it takes creativity and persistence. One of our first graders, for example, had not only not learned to read, but quickly crawled under her desk whenever a book or worksheet was offered!

It was clear that we needed to try another approach. The answer came through a game called Hop 'n' Stomp, which included small belts,

Who ran to help me when I fell,
And would some pretty story tell,
Or kiss the place to make it well?
My mother.
ANN TAYLOR & JUNE TAYLOR, *MY MOTHER*

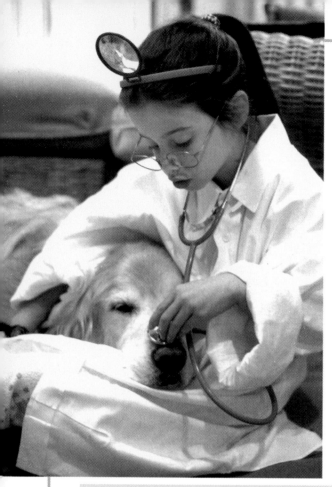

with suction cups attached at the bottom, that buckled around a child's shoes. The game also included plastic disks printed with the letters of the alphabet, that were tossed randomly on the carpet.

Our reluctant reader enjoyed hopping and stomping around the room, picking up the disks with her special "shoes." As she retrieved several disks, she removed them from the suction cups and named each letter as she handed it to her teacher. Then she went merrily on her way gathering more letters, beaming like a star in the sky.

In time, the letters were replaced with patterns and words. The day came when she mastered the words on the disks, and a book was

once again placed on her desk. This time, however, she didn't push it away or crawl under the desk, because now she was able to read. What a great victory for her! Like every girl, like every child, her uniqueness allowed her to succeed in her own special way.

The same was true for a young lady who graduated from our school for children with learning disabilities and was accepted into a fine academy. At the end of September, in her freshman year, I received a phone call from the principal of the academy. At first, I thought our former student might be having trouble achieving in the mainstream. My doubts and fears soon vanished as the principal shared her story.

During study hall, the girls were permitted to choose their study partners, and everyone sought out our young graduate. Not only was she organized, but she displayed a special ability for helping her partners get

They walked along listening to the singing of the bright-colored birds and looking at the lovely flowers which now became so thick that the ground was carpeted with them.
L. FRANK BAUM, *THE WONDERFUL WIZARD OF OZ*

organized and complete their assignments. Although it would have been easy to imagine that with her learning disability, she would require special help, the opposite turned out to be true.

In adapting to life's challenges and struggles, young girls discover how to deal with difficult problems. They learn that it's acceptable to disagree agreeably, that it's okay to have their own opinions, and for others to have different ones. Young girls need to unravel the mysteries of life for themselves, by experimenting and experiencing, by making mistakes and learning from them, by testing friendships and by trusting their own feelings. ✳

Stay is a charming word in a friend's vocabulary.
LOUISA MAY ALCOTT

A TIME FOR BLOSSOMING

One needn't go far to discover the remarkable world a girl creates, not just for herself, but for others. Life opens its mysteries to her, and she is eager to explore the heights and depths of the universe.

Her vision is boundless. She reaches toward the unknown, cautious but unafraid, confident that she'll find a safe haven where her trust and

I celebrate myself, and sing myself.
WALT WHITMAN, *SONG OF MYSELF*

confidence can grow. She'll tug at your hand and lead you to new and exciting adventures as ordinary as building a castle in the sand, or watching the stars come out, or naming shapes in the clouds. Everything is new to her—and her enthusiastic exploration of her world can help revive the wonder of it in *your* heart and soul.

Today, young girls are making their own decisions, following their own dreams, and working toward their own goals—learning how to become the person *they* want to be. Stereotypes don't cast shadows on the sun in their universe. New careers beckon. New role models abound, and lifelong dreams can be achieved. They can reach whichever star they choose and, with persistence and determination, attain their heart's desires.

My friend's grandchild, for example, loves animals. She'd take any stray or wounded bird or animal and bring it home to her little hospital. With a loving

You must do the things you think you cannot do.
ELEANOR ROOSEVELT

heart and tender care, she nursed them back to health and found homes for them. Her innate compassion and gentleness helped her decide her life's work—she wants to be a veterinarian. Now she volunteers her time and talents at the local animal shelter.

To paraphrase one of my favorite quotations: A happy girlhood lasts a lifetime. How true! If every girl expresses her uniqueness by continuously testing the boundaries of her imagination, then she will have a happy girlhood. And her happiness as a woman will be a certainty.

You see things and you say, "Why?" But I dream things that never were and I say, "Why not?"
GEORGE BERNARD SHAW

When so rich a harvest is before us, why do we not gather it? All is in our hands if we will but use it.
ELIZABETH ANN SETON, FIRST AMERICAN SAINT

Young girls blossom when all the elements we have touched on come together—their individual uniqueness, their capacity for loving and for being loved, their independent values and sense of character, and their ability to accept responsibility and stand for what they believe in.

Young girls blossom when least expected, in unexpected ways, despite the obstacles that stand, or that we think stand, in their way. By celebrating and encouraging our girls' high aspirations, enthusiasm, and strong desire to succeed, we ensure the world of a future Madame Curie, Eleanor Roosevelt, Rosa Park,

No coward soul is mine.
EMILY BRONTË, *LAST LINES*

Mother Teresa, Harriet Tubman, and Susan B. Anthony.

The world becomes a better place when innocent young girls grow up to be generous and loving young women. Their sparkling wit and sensitive humor can open our eyes and hearts to realms beyond our everyday existence. They are the flower in the arid land, the bright star in the sky, the hope in the darkness, and the future of all our tomorrows.

Be good, sweet maid, and let who can be clever; Do noble things, not dream them, all day long.
CHARLES KINGSLEY, *A FAREWELL*

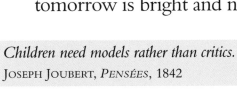

This is our reward for the examples we've set, and the approvals we've offered. Our support makes it possible for our young girls to shatter any limits and overcome any obstacles that might stand in their paths.

Ah, the world is a better place because of little girls! But let us help them grow into the mature, responsible, caring, and giving leaders of the generations to come. That is our legacy—one that they will embrace with a full heart and soul as they continue their journey through life. The world will grow with them—and learn from them that tomorrow is bright and new! *

Children need models rather than critics.
JOSEPH JOUBERT, *PENSÉES*, 1842

O world, I cannot hold thee close enough!
EDNA ST. VINCENT MILLAY
"GOD'S WORLD," *RENASCENE*, 1973

PERMISSIONS

I am woman, hear me roar.
HELEN REDDY